LEADERSHIP'S
TOP 12

UNLEASH THE GREATNESS WITHIN YOU

"Leaders are ordinary people who are just like you and me.
The only difference is that
GREAT LEADERS
have a sense of Duty that allows them
to rise above their circumstances, problems, situations
and even their own self interests,
in order
to promote a level of influence
that is worthy of imitating."

Sharon D. Green
Certified Leadership Expert

Leadership's Top 12: Unleash the Greatness Within You

Copyright © 2013 by Alethes Consulting Group

Printed in United States of America

ISBN: 978-0-9889432-0-9

Foreward

When people come into your life for a season, it is usually to meet a need you have expressed outwardly or inwardly. They may come to assist you through difficulty, to provide you with guidance and support, to aid you physically, emotionally, or spiritually. They are there to meet a need.

Then without any wrongdoing on your part, they will say or do something to bring the relationship to an end. In some cases this may involve death, and in other cases it is a result of a choice to walk away. It's other times they may act in a certain way that forces you to take a stand. However, in reality, the need has been met and a season has come to an end.

There are other people who come into your life for a lifetime. They come to share, grow or add value to your existence. Their experiences may provide a sense of peace or make you laugh. Through their life, you learn things that you have never thought of or accomplished. These friendships usually provide an unbelievable amount of joy, as pain is overshadowed by love.

Lifetime relationships are what you build upon in order to have a solid emotional foundation. You grow to accept the lessons, unconditionally love the person, and take what you learn from the relationship and apply it to all the other areas of your life.

Sharon Green is truly a lifetime friend. A living, walking example of focus, discipline, determination, leadership and love. To know Sharon and see her live life with purpose is truly amazing, exciting and exhilarating. She is constantly learning and teaching, uplifting everyone that listens. Her accomplishments are many but her love for others is undeniably her purpose for living. This book is just one example of her leadership and provides the love that lasts, and found only in the truth.

Humble yourselves therefore under the mighty hand of God, that he may exalt you in due time.

(1PETER 5:6)

Thank you for supporting my lifetime sister-friend. Her time has come…. Hallelujah!!!

Wanda Michals

TABLE OF CONTENTS

"Leadership is not title, position, power or stature, it is influence, nothing more, nothing less."

JOHN C. MAXWELL

INTRODUCTION

A Leader's ability to influence self is the key fundamental principle required for great results. You are a Leader, created for victory. You were not created to be average. Therefore, you must be a Leader of one (You), before you can lead any-1. You have what it takes for success; it's already inside of you awaiting your attention and proper use. Greatness is available, making you the most suited person for your passion and purpose.

What type of Leader are you? Who are you following? Would **you** follow you? Leadership is so much more than just being confident that you can manage people and make them follow your instructions. Each one of us will influence thousands of people during our lifetime in addition to family and friends. Therefore, the companion question to whether or not you would follow you, as clearly you have the ability to influence; is, in what manner are you influencing you and others?

Character, Integrity and Ethical behavior are key characteristics of Leaders, especially global Leaders of the future. Making these characteristics key throughout all spectrums of leadership. Great value has been placed on these attributes, as they appear to be sorely lacking in many Leaders. On the contrary, the key to effective leadership does not only depend on the abilities you are born with, or your inner personality, or from your philosophy of leadership, but it is found in techniques, skills, and qualities that you are open to develop throughout life. Leadership is cultivated by your enthusiasm to become the person other people will follow. How you react when your power or safety is challenged, and how you interpret the world around you, is crucial to developing strong and effective leadership qualities.

Existing and future Leaders of the world, this book is designed to help you identify and develop those Leadership qualities lying dormant within you, and increase your personal and professional success. Whether your desire is to lead a student body, your children, start a business, or pastor a congregation, the first step in achieving greatness is to develop and discipline the Leader that is already inside of you.

Are you ready? Let's get started and countdown Leadership's Top 12 qualities while cultivating your greatness, enhancing your awareness, and producing awesome results in every area of your life. All of which will make undeniable impact in the lives of those that you lead!

"To Add Growth, Lead Followers...To Multiply, Lead Leaders"

JOHN C. MAXWELL

COMING IN AT (12)

A Leader Must Be Able to
DEVELOP OTHER LEADERS

This quality is actually an ability; however, it's the combination of the other qualities and the Leader's ability to see leadership potential in others that actually develops Leaders. Some of the proudest moments in a parent's life are when they are blessed to celebrate their children's successes. Leadership is no different for those of us who strive to make a difference in the lives of those that we lead. When the people around you flourish and grow, that is a clear reflection of your leadership. When the people around you then become impactful Leaders that is a reflection of your legacy.

When a Leader fails to develop other leaders, is when the Leader finds themselves doing all of the thinking and all of the work. This approach to Leadership is unnecessary, especially since the purpose of leading is to lead people. So why the need to develop followers into Leaders who are capable of making an impact? Even babies are expected to crawl, walk, run and eventually move out of your house. Once again, followers are

5

no different; growth must take place with a goal of producing Leaders who reflect the qualities of their teacher. Becoming a Leader who develops Leaders not only produces substantial growth, it requires a different mindset. John Maxwell's philosophy is that "There is no success without a successor."

Will your successor represent the same qualities that you possess or will they represent their own self-interests. What is received from the Leader is what the follower will reflect. Developing and leading Leaders requires that you not be me-focused and reward centered. You must operate on a level of love that always gives and seeks ways to improve upon the talents of another; without requiring anything personal in return. You must manage your expectations, as the up-and-coming Leader is not you, and may not have strengths in certain areas that you deem as common practice. You must be patient. You must be confident that you are worth imitating. You must be optimistic that people capable of leading others are available and all around you. You must be selective and devote your energy to those who have potential and desire to make the same focused impact in the lives of the people that they lead as you do. You must be confident with no ulterior motive that may jeopardize your efforts and transfer the wrong qualities to your Leaders. Here are some great methods to help you develop Leaders.

BRINGING OUT THE LEADER'S LEADER IN YOU

Every Leader should have a coach on the sideline. Since you now represent the coach, know that those you're looking to lead cannot rise above your level of leadership. Therefore, make sure that you have a coach/mentor/someone adding to and correcting weaknesses in your leadership efforts. Who would not want to have a Heisman Quarterback and a back-up quarterback who has the same awareness, skills, athleticism, knowledge and understanding as the starting quarterback. Well it's the coach who is instrumental in recruiting, building the team and calling the plays. The quarterback may be the Leader on the field, but it definitely provides comfort for him/her to receive and reflect wise counsel from the sideline. As the coach, it is now your duty to develop Leaders who can lead in your presence and in your absence.

1. **Be a good listener.** Most people never receive instructions on how to listen. The message is normally lost in translation when the meaning is misunderstood. It does not help that we hear from where we are unconsciously located. For example, people with low self-esteem will always hear from a place of 'me.' If you were to ask this person when was the next time that they were getting their hair done. They would hear, "I look a mess." However, the question was intended to obtain a date so that you could possibly pay the bill and reward the person for their outstanding contribution to the organization. Communication is not communication until it's understood by both parties.

Good Leaders are great listeners. They possess the ability to hear above their own knowledge and be open to receive a new thought as a result of communicating. Leaders give their people the opportunity to express their viewpoints and ask questions in order to receive complete meaning of what is being said. Hearing is not the same as listening. I can personally tell you of numerous meetings that I sat through, heard the information, but since I was not listening, I could not take notes. If you have children, you have witnessed this skill-set (LoL) and know exactly what I am referring to. How often do you have to ask your children, "What did I just say." I jokingly referred to this ability as a skill set, but it's the inability to focus that makes hearing and listening two different activities. This is why focused listening adds success both to you and to the development of your people. When you listen as your people express their ideas and opinions, you actually are giving them a chance to consider themselves as a valuable asset and contribute to the organization's growth. Each engagement where you listen, appreciate and give your people credit for their great ideas and/or feedback, you encourage open communication and tear down the barriers that sometimes are in place between Leader and follower.

2. **Be concerned.** Great Leaders understand that the team's commitment is the root source for his/her

dreams being realized, and therefore, renders genuine care and concern for each team member's well-being. This concern also flows into his/her immediate family. It shows itself by remembering names of followers, their spouses and possibly children too. It celebrates birthdays and anniversaries, and recognizes those times in life where followers may be happy and/or sad. It is the personal touches that allow followers to connect to the Leader's heart.

Concern is also displayed when the Leader takes responsibility for their actions, renders appropriate affirming discipline, defends his team before others, helps out when circumstances appear to be impossible, and provides food and hope for those long extra hours of work. It is displayed in and outside of the work environment.

Things that seem to be of no importance to you might be extremely critical to your people. You must be able to empathize with their needs.

3. **Learn to motivate.** You are your team's biggest cheerleader. If you have no confidence in your people, it is your fault. Leadership requires the ability to solve problems; therefore, if your problem is found in incompetent followers who you have not trained then you are the problem. If your problem is undisciplined followers who have not received corrective action - you

are the problem. It's hard to motivate people that you have no confidence in. Motivate your problem folks with affirming corrective training and if that doesn't work, terminate and replace them with others who will add value to your organization. As the Leader, always do your part first to ensure that your people are given every opportunity to succeed.

You have the ability to inspire your people to work towards common goals and to achieve things they never thought they could do. Learn how to motivate by exploring different ideas and needs. You must recognize that the same rewards do not motivate everyone. Motivation is not limited to rewards. Your words and actions have a lasting value that rewards just do not have. Simple statements like, "You're doing a great job...I appreciate you." can change the low self-esteem person's entire perspective on life.

However, do not confuse motivation with manipulation. Motivation occurs when you persuade others to take an action in their own best interests, while manipulation is persuading others to take an action that is primarily for your benefit. Leaders and motivators are winners; manipulators are losers who produce resentment and dispute. Become a motivator, lead your people, and never manipulate them for your own personal gain.

4. **Invest Time in Others.** As you develop Leaders, you must empower and assist others to achieve their full potential. This is where you focus the 80% of your time and resources to develop the gifts of the top 20% of your closest Leaders. Capitalizing on their strengths and developing their weaknesses will not only develop leadership within your organization, but it has the potential to multiply leadership that will impact the lives of people that you may never know. Share personal knowledge and insight that will propel your people past struggles, through their challenges and into the successes that lie ahead. The more time that you invest in others, the greater the return on investment.

5. **Challenge them!** Purposefully plan challenging, exciting, and meaningful assignments for your Leaders to resolve. Don't hesitate to ask your Leaders for their opinion and stretch them to master their own leadership concerns. Once you see them successfully leading before success actually takes place, you will eliminate the sympathetic desire to not push them out of their comfort zone when the excuses start flying. It's the challenges that Leaders overcome that help to solidify their value as a Leader.

6. **Continue to develop you. I cannot stress this point enough;** Leaders are learners. Although you may have the gift to develop other Leaders, Great Leaders who

produce Great Leaders never max out on knowledge. Growth is intentional; it does not just happen. Once you, the Leader/Coach/Mentor, continue to grow, you keep the knowledge flowing through the pipeline, just like the root system of a tree. Plant wisely; a healthy root system equals a healthy tree; a healthy Leader multiplies great leadership through the lives of others.

"There are only 24 hours in each day, my priority is to deliberately manage me so that I may maximize productivity in time, in order to maximize daily results."

COMING IN AT 11

A Leader Must Be Deliberate

Leadership comes with a great deal of responsibility that requires a deliberate programming, planning, prioritizing and executing. People often add a mix to leadership that is oftentimes unpredictable. The diversity of daily requirements must have a priority of effort if the Leader ever expects to get anything accomplished. If you are experiencing challenges as a Leader, it may be that your competing requirements are telling you what to do instead of you doing the leading.

Leaders must be deliberate and disciplined to prioritize while working towards specific goals. Knowing the what, when, where, why and how will make life as a Leader more consistent and focused. Being deliberate forces Leaders to prioritize or rank order, all of the competing requirements that must be accomplished, by importance. I've found that a great way to prioritize is by strategic planning and by using the Pareto Principle known as the 20/80 principle, to narrow the scope of effort.

Strategizing or defining the organizational plan as it supports the vision requires specification. Strategic planning is the roadmap for success. Unfortunately, describing the entities involved in strategic planning make for a book in and of itself. Therefore, if you require additional information in this area of leadership, use the sign up information located at the back of this book and take advantage of your FREE 30 minute consultation. Please know that leadership requires strategic planning in order to achieve successful engagements, so do not blow it off. Meanwhile, here is a powerful nugget from a famous bear, named Yogi Berra: "If you don't know where you are going, you will wind up somewhere else."

The Pareto Principle states that 20 percent of your priorities will give you 80 percent of production. The remaining 80% of results are achieved with only 20% of the effort. This principle applies to people, as well as, organizational requirements. For example, if you rank order 10 people that work directly for you where your number one person is truly your number one producer, and your number two is truly your number two producer, and number three is truly your 3rd best producer through 10; the Pareto Principle states that maximum effort/personal development given to the top two people (20%) will produce a 80% return on investment

Now that you know where to focus your attention, in order to prioritize correctly you must first organize. Each and every task may be classified in 4 categories:

➤ **High Important and High Urgency**: Should be top priority.

➤ **High Importance and Low Urgency**: Use deadlines for completion and accomplish within the daily routine.

➤ **Low Importance and High Urgency**: Seek ways to accomplish with minimal disruption of the daily routine, but with a quick solution that may be given to an assistant.

➤ **Low Importance and Low Urgency**: Normally busy repetitive work that keeps order, but not necessarily a daily requirement. Designate time and work on acquiring automation that may eliminate it all together.

Effective leadership and management also include knowing how to say "NO." This means saying NO to others and to self. Restricting yourself from doing unimportant tasks will grant you more time to focus on the more important requirements. One important requirement is to ensure that your leadership team is prioritizing their efforts as well.

As a Leader, you must also be able to identify the things that require the most attention. The Leader's competence and ability to get things done when apparent to the Followers, increases their confidence in not only your ability to lead, but in your ability to produce the right results. The team develops a greater awareness of the direction that the Leader is leading and become active participants in the Leader's vision.

BRINGING OUT THE ORGANIZED AND SYSTEMATIZED YOU

In his book *Leadership 101*, John Maxwell reminds all Leaders: "Remember: It's not how hard you work; it's how smart you work. The ability to juggle three or four high priority projects successfully is a must for every Leader." So how can you become a more organized Leader?

1. **Make assessments.** Ask, "Is this the best use of me in time right now?" With so many things you ought to do, having a set limit of time in each day, make every moment of you in time, useful. Categorize, analyze and prioritize every task to determine importance and the time required to complete each task. Make appropriate choices as determined by your assessment. Another great assessment tool is to use the A.C.T principle: A = Action, C = Change, T = Teach. Categorize requirements by whether or not they require action, change or are worthy of teaching. Once you've completed your categories, organize and prioritize each item in the appropriate category and rank order. Example: A1, A2, A3..., C1, C2, C3...T1, T2, T3...

2. **Make a to-do list.** Visual aids add value and are great reminders of what is and is not important. In your list,

make sure your tasks are listed according to priorities, or you can simply rank them according to their importance (for example, 5 is the most important task and 1 is the least important task).

3. **Say NO to things that undermine your goals and vision.** Priorities are designed to identify and direct effort. Every now and then, something and someone comes along that may present an opportunity to divert your attention away from your maximum effort. During these times, you must remain focused just like a horse running the Kentucky Derby. Put on your blinders, continue looking straight ahead and resist the temptation to say YES. Do not visualize what is during these times visualize what can be. These times also require that you exercise balance when considering family and friends who may not understand. I recommend that you pray first then say NO, knowing that Leaders never replace family with work. We work for the benefit of the family; which must have the proper balance that is only fortified through lack of proper communication.

4. **Stop procrastinating.** Instead agreeing to something else now and finishing your work later;" try changing your confession to "I'll finish my work now so that I may do something else later." Procrastination is the enemy to productivity. Ridding yourself of this popular, yet horrible, leadership trait is just a matter

of choice. You can choose to be efficient and effective. You can choose to be a better manager of yourself and in time that time may be maximized as a product of your efforts. It all starts in your mind. When you think like a finisher, you finish. The more that you practice being a finisher, the more that procrastination will be a thing of the past.

5. **Love what you do, do what you love and make it known.** When you truly love what you do, you lead effortlessly. You wake up excited and you go to bed expecting. Your attitude provides an awareness by all that the vision being supported is connected to GREAT. Your confidence is strengthened and pursuit of more, better and right become contagious. When this occurs, even the things that you hate to do become effortless.

6. **Don't be a perfectionist.** Be deliberate. This is definitely one of my greatest leadership challenges. Because I am someone who thinks highly of herself, not more highly than I should, but just highly of myself, this gives me great awareness of how people and things represent me in my absence. Therefore, I tend to ensure that not only results are achieved, but that the right results are achieved. This sounds good, but sometimes this form of thinking delays progress that could have taken place while waiting for the perfect ending to matter. I have no plans of denying

my perfectionist frame of thinking, but I've grown to accept OK, when OK gets the job done. My advice to you is that you too, should think highly of yourself, enforcing standards and correction when and where needed. Choose quality. Set standards early on and be consistent so that your people will know what to expect as they imitate and represent you in your absence.

"Change will not come if we wait for some other person or some other time. We are the ones we've been waiting for. We are the change that we seek."

PRESIDENT BARAK OBAMA

COMING IN AT 10

A Leader Must Be ADAPTABLE

Although deliberate in effort, Leaders must remain adaptable by nature. Adaptability in this chapter refers to being willing to change. It does not mean to conform to the status quo. A great Leader knows how to adjust, adapt and overcome; they are willing to make necessary changes for the right reasons and for the good of the team. It is when Leaders fully understand their ability to impact their environment, that the environment is forced to submit to the leading of the "Agent of Change." Otherwise, you are merely one of the followers.

As previously stated throughout this book, leadership requires that the Leader grow. Growth requires change. Change is not always pleasant, and therefore, requires analysis to determine if it is necessary. When change is dictated by a higher entity, necessity takes a back seat to obedience.

Throughout my military career, I've had several opportunities to serve as an Agent of Change These occurrences always seem to involve more work with less people. If I would have fallen victim to the numerous complaints, the impact that I was able to make as the Leader would have been undermined. Instead, I made it known that our circumstances would not dictate our outcome, I asked for their support and I answered questions/concerns. I also followed up with the necessary changes that would streamline processes, eliminating those non-value-added, "we've always done it this way," things that provided extra work and no results. Today, I can proudly say that from the days of my first Army officer assignment when my impending boss, who I never met in person, was diagnosed with Cancer and died, making me the boss, through my senior officer years where I reorganized a full service Army finance office from approximately 90 people to 30, deployed a team of 12 to Cuba with no guidance, and reorganized pay processes for a deployed Finance battalion of over 200 people, in order to support a 17,000 person division with approximately 35 people, I had zero occurrences where success was not achieved. Yes I did have a few rebellious folks who were disgruntled about the added workload, but I was able to love them, through correction, back into agreement where their actions did not bleed over into the productive folks. These successes only occurred because I embraced change early in the process, and confidently transferred the same vision to those who remained.

Some Leaders do not make changes because they try to conform to what is normal. They are afraid to step out of the comfort zone; they lack imagination. What they do not realize is that normal is growing and adapting to new and different without them. They are stuck in the world of being efficient. Efficiency is to do what's right. However, they are missing out on the world of being effective. Effectiveness means to do the right things. This is what keeps them efficient yet ineffective.

Leaders must be willing to create positive change, even when change requires personal loss. You can only reproduce who you are. Therefore, once you are willing to change, then your organization and those around you will change. Be different. Set the example in industry. Continuously seeking better and improved ways to do something should be the norm. It is genius and will place you on top of your industry faster. Leadership does not require public approval, but public approval will be granted as successful results are consistently achieved. Embrace change and remain willing to adapt and overcome.

"It is not the strongest of the species that survives, nor the most intelligent that survives. It is the one that is the most adaptable to change."

CHARLES DARWIN

BRINGING OUT THE CHANGE-MAKER IN YOU

"Positive changes in your life will not be finished today, but it can start today," says David Niven, Ph. D., author of *The 100 Simple Secrets of Success*.

Here are some techniques on how to handle change properly:

1. **Be creative.** Whether it's a free lunch from somebody who arrives late in a meeting, or a song and dance when a simple errand was forgotten, new and fun rules can make everyone's work exciting. Let your mind work and produce imaginative new stuffs. Before you know it, no one will be arriving late any more and all errands will be finished on time.

2. **Take risks.** Put your faith to work early on by changing your conversation. Say what you want to see while you put your hands to the plow. Wise counsel and calculated risk will help eliminate the fear of failure.

3. **Continue to learn.** Find out what is working for your competitors and do not be afraid to ask them questions. Make them tell you NO. The messenger with your answer has no limits, so be open to the message, and do not judge the messenger. Attend meetings, conferences, events where you are the dumbest person in the room. Ask questions and take notes. Take the lid off of your leadership and seek out people capable of giving you an original thought. From new thoughts and ideas that you have gathered, develop new policies and procedures and make the right decisions for you and your people.

4. **Say no to the status quo.** John Maxwell describes Leaders as "never content with things as they are." Additionally, he says that leading, by definition, is to be in front, breaking new ground, conquering new worlds, moving away from the status quo. New isn't new until it's different from the old.

"It is not about what was said, as much as it is about what you heard."

DR. MICHAEL A. FREEMAN

COMING IN AT ⑨

A LEADER MUST BE AN EFFECTIVE
COMMUNICATOR

Communication is the key to knowing, understanding and achieving success. An effective Leader must develop communication skills in order to communicate and connect with followers. It's not so much your ability to speak as it is your ability to be heard and responded to. It's not so much your ability to hear, as it is your ability to effectively listen and see.

President Gerald Ford once said, "*Nothing in life is more important than the ability to communicate effectively.*" This is because without effective communication, a Leader is just speaking words. Relationship demands effective communication. Casting your vision and holding others accountable to their part in achieving the vision demands effective communication. Parenting demands effective communication. You know that you are communicating and connecting when your children hear, receive and do what you communicate the first time it's heard.

In many ways, effective communication begins with mutual respect. It inspires, encourages, and motivates others to do their best. When Leaders appear to respect their people, you, as the Leader will never appear rude, even during correction. Consequently, by giving respect, you get enthusiasm, cooperation, and voluntary participation. It's amazing how the right words, heard, can change the atmosphere of an entire organization.

Once the Leader is seen favorably in the eyes of those following, the followers will gain a desire to assist you even in areas outside of their area of responsibility. Effective communication has the power to take the obligation out of work. It fortifies unity of effort and builds rapport and confidence in your ability to lead and make a difference.

Communication is groomed out of our ability to listen. Most people just want to be heard, recognized as being important. Therefore, listening only to gain access to the conversation with no regard for the thoughts and opinions that are being voiced by another is unacceptable. Effective listening is a skill, just like effective communication, that goes in two directions. It is the listeners responsibility to hear right, as it is the person speaking responsibility to formulate words that may be understood.

BRINGING OUT THE EFFECTIVE COMMUNICATOR IN YOU

Effective communication is not just about the words that we speak, but it is more about ensuring that those words are understood as if the other person were saying the exact same thing. Understanding takes place in words that are received thorough body language, tone, inflection, pronunciation, volume, speed of delivery, confidence in material, presentation of presenter, facial expression; it all speaks at the same time. The goal is to make sure that all of these elements are saying the same thing.

The one thing that I stress to my son when we have our moments of "my hands were made to love," is that "your body language speaks louder than your words." I'm teaching him to be a Leader at a young age, which requires his understanding that **disrespect and honor are seen first and heard second.**

If you have children, then you understand why they are a great resource for testing your communication skills. Children hear from where they are at; they hear from a place that competes with how they feel at the time of communication. You find yourself saying, "What did I just say?" If your children are anything like mines, and you've taught them not to lie, then you've experienced their humble eye contact as they laughingly say, "I don't know." This response is normally followed by their attempt to summarize the entire conversation in the last words that were spoken.

Here are a few ways to develop effective communication skills:

1. **Discuss, don't argue.** Great Leaders value the opinions of others. Therefore, during times of disagreement, we discuss, ask questions and listen. This is also a time of reassessment in times of uncertainty. Leaders explain

calmly and have the confidence required to not allow the actions of others to move them into a place of regret. Proverbs 15:1 advises us that, "A soft answer turns away wrath, but a harsh word stirs up anger."

2. **Focus as the speaker.** When the focus is primarily towards self and getting your opinion across, effective communication is easily lost in translation. To be a good communicator, talk to people, not above or below them. State your point, repeat the important things; allow the response of the people to lead you forward or backward in your communication. Don't hesitate to ask questions in order to ensure that a connection is being made.

3. **Learn to listen.** Active listening produces more than just understanding. It allows you to hear the heartbeat of another; it provides vision for trust, and reveals their level of sincerity. Effective listening allows you to 'see' what the other person is saying. Although, TV is expensive and combines audio and visual to produce a greater sales impact, radio advertisement being less expensive, airs the message more frequently, painting a picture on the canvas of the listener's imagination that is visible as if seen with their two eyes. Allow others to speak openly, and as the Leader, listen to see. Guide your people when they're off and stretch them when they're on.

4. **Develop eye contact while communicating.** Eye contact during communication develops confidence, integrity and conviction. It physically shows that you are interested and willing to actively participate in the conversation.

5. **Never forget to smile.** They say that it takes 47 muscles to frown, but only 17 to smile. A simple, sincere smile has the power to enhance likeability, it relieves unnecessary tension and dismisses preconceived opinions. Besides spending less effort for such a greater reward, smiling will open the lines of communication and welcome other people to join the conversation. Maxwell reminds, "A smile overcomes innumerable communication barriers, crossing the boundaries of culture, race, age, class, gender, education, and economic status."

Leaders rise and fall by the decisions we make.

COMING IN AT 8

A LEADER MUST BE DECISIVE

Having served 23 years in the military, the one leadership trait that caused me to have physical unrest was a superior Leader's inability to make a decision. It is imperative for a Leader to make a decision and take responsibility for that decision. It is the example of integrity that keeps great leaders making the right decisions for the right reason at the right time. President Theodore Roosevelt says it this way, "*In any moment of decision the best thing you can do is the right thing, the next best thing is the wrong thing, and the worst thing you can do is nothing.*" People are looking to you, the Leader, to make a decision. This is not always an easy place to reside.

During my military career, I deployed a team of Soldiers, Non-Commissioned Officers and Commissioned Officers to Guantanamo-Bay, Cuba. I trained to deploy, but actually had no desire to deploy in support of a unit for which I was not assigned. Days prior to the deployment, after coming to terms with my inevitable assignment, I was asked by team members what we were to accomplish while in Cuba. I had to make a decision: make the team feel secure about deploying or tell them the truth. This is what I shared with my team, *"I don't know...but whatever we are supposed to do, we will do it and come back home."* I immediately received the Army call-sign for OK, *HOOAH*, and we prepared to deploy. Why did this happen with such confidence, and without the fear found in uncertainty. It was a relatively easy victory because of my ability to influence others, having a reputation for being a decision maker and problem solver in a financial management industry where we serviced thousands of customers daily. This turned out to be an amazingly successful deployment for all involved in spite of the fact that I, the Leader, led strangers into a foreign land of uncertainty. The majority of the team was meeting me up close and in person for the first time, but once again, it was my reputation for being technically proficient, decisive and a person of integrity who genuinely cares for others that they heard about and grew to know. However, I know that it was my ability to always tell the truth that far outweighed any emotional decision to make everyone comfortable with a lie.

Decision-making comes with great responsibility. It is your responsibility to use your power for good. Leadership is not too different from being superheroes that also have followers that look to them for hope. Yes, you may not have served in the military or have super powers like Superman, Batman and Spiderman, but you have the authority and ability to lead and develop people towards success. This is such a greater responsibility since your decisions contain the power to impact the lives of real people who trust you as their Leader. Hence, Leaders must not only be able to make a decision, but they must make the right decision at the right time.

Who said it is easy to be a Leader? Some say, it is not...I say, those people are doing something wrong. The challenge of leading life with so much responsibility and reward, far outweigh the setbacks. Besides, it's a set-back and not a stay-back, so come back and conquer the next challenge with an expectation of winning. True Leaders are willing to accept them all. There are instances where sometimes it makes us feel better to blame somebody or something else when situations and circumstances do not go according to plan. However, this is the easy way out and definitely a sign of a leadership deficit that should not be practiced.

A Leader should take full responsibility for the decisions made within his/her organization. This is only realistic when the will of the Leader is known. As much as you are responsible for the organization's success, you are also responsible for any failure. In instances of failure, it is your responsibility as the Leader to implement counseling, correction and reprimand as needed. You are the catalyst of change. Decisions that result in failure have a source, it is your responsibility to identify the source and make decisions that will produce future favorable results. Even the right decisions in lieu of failure, provide the potential to learn and grow.

BRINGING OUT THE DECISION-MAKER IN YOU

Sometimes, require some assistance to defeat the doubts that discourage our self-worth and ability to make decisions. However, knowledge combined with confidence supports your ability to look within, make the right decisions and take responsibility for the results. Below is a list of how to draw the Decision-Maker out of you:

1. **Develop self-awareness.** As a Leader, you should know your own strengths and weaknesses in order to access your ability to make decisions. Remain open to feedback, and make changes when necessary. When you have awareness and are true to yourself, you are better equipped as a whole to know and understand what tasks you should engage in, and what situations you are not equipped to handle single-handedly.

   Dr. Gerald Bell, business consultant and professor at the University of North Carolina, Chapel Hill, N.C, advises us on how to expand our self-knowledge, *"Study yourself closely and practice self-assessment techniques to learn how you behave and the effects you have on others. Ask others for their opinions or criticisms and what you can do to become a better Leader."*

2. **Do not equate decision-making with worry.** When decisions are required and we hear the word responsibility, we often think to ourselves, "Another task; another problem!" However, responsibility is

more than worrying about things given to us to work out. Decision Making is opportunity -- opportunity to make a difference in your organization and in the lives of others. Consider this short story:

One night at the end of the second shift, an employee walked out and passed the Night Manager setting at his desk. As head of operations, the Night Manager had started his day at the beginning of the first shift, and maintained responsibility for the evening shift too. The employee as he departed said, "Mr. Jones, I sure wish I had your pay, but I don't want your worry."

The employee equated responsibility (decision-making) with worry. Clearly the employee's priority was self. He had no understanding of using his many hours at work to make an impact on the lives of others.

Let's say that the vice-president of a prestigious company and the employee are paid the same money, who would you want to be? Being the decision maker with responsibility should never intimidate you, because of the joy of accomplishment – the feeling of helping other people – is what Leadership is all about. You must know that the reward of great leadership has multiplication value in the lives that are impacted by your leadership.

3. **Take risks.** Effective Leaders have the courage to act in situations where results and success are uncertain.

They are willing to risk failure. In doing this, you always have to be prepared. Analyze the situation, your options and known variables. List the pros and the cons for each choice and perform a risk analysis. Perform a risk analysis by assigning each choice a risk factor ranking from 1 to 5. Next, determine the likelihood that each outcome will occur. This will help you know how much risk you are willing to take.

Seek perfection, but know that there may be unknown variables that may skew your results.

4. **Be ready to admit your mistakes.** Everyone makes mistakes. It is normal. Avoid making excuses and blaming others for something you did wrong. Admitting your mistakes and failures will even make people respect you more, as you are being true to yourself. It's not the mistakes, it's how you handle the mistakes that matter.

"Attitude is the measure of what is in your heart."

COMING IN AT 7

A LEADER MUST HAVE
A POSITIVE ATTITUDE

Earl Nightingale, in his book, *Lead from the Field*, defines attitude as "the position or bearing as indicating action, feeling or mood; and it is our actions, feelings and mood that determines the action, feeling and mood of others towards us." As a Leader, you must have a positive attitude towards yourself in order to project a positive attitude towards others. It's impossible to give others what you do not have. In his book, *Developing the Leaders around You*, my mentor, John Maxwell describes his view of a positive attitude as "one of the most valuables assets a person can have in life." The beauty of attitude is that it's already inside of you, and you can control it.

Attitude can help you achieve things that may seem impossible at first. It moves you from thought to action, and allows you to see the end at the beginning. Attitude is a choice. You can choose to live life by default or by design. It's up to you to take responsibility for your thoughts, feelings, actions and words.

As a Leader, your attitude is just as important as your know how. I strongly recommend that you take time regularly to check your attitude, before it gets checked. When faced with adversity, it is your attitude that will either affect panic or peace. You choose. Yet at the end of the day remain engaged, excited, satisfied and optimistic that the solution is at hand.

Most of the time, we become discouraged by how difficult the problem appears, taking our eyes off of the solution. What we must understand is that it's not the problems of life that are difficult to deal with, but rather our attitude towards them. There may not always be a quick fix, but with the right attitude, the long fix will appear resolved as optimism keeps the solution in focus in lieu of the problem.

I'm not leading you into denial, but am reminding you of your ability to choose. Your attitude is a key indicator of what you will get out of life. Depending on what you would like to achieve, attitude is also the barometer of how long it will take you to climb, to reach your full potential. Think about it, a mountain climber does not look for a lot of gear to carry up the mountain, but remains content with the supplies required for the journey knowing that extra weight adds extra pain. The more that the climber's attention remains on carrying supplies, the more likely he/she will lighten the load by discarding items along the way. The problem with lightening the load prematurely is that it places the climber in a disadvantage with miles to go before reaching the top, having to descend on the other side of the mountain with no supplies. Descending has proven just as dangerous as climbing. Attitude in this scenario allowed a temporary occurrence to produce potentially long-term physical results.

See the big picture. Look beyond the problem. A positive Leader will not dwell on a difficult situation and be discouraged by it, but will believe that he can and he ought to surpass it in order to reach his goals. With a positive attitude, he never accepts defeat. Instead, he fights the noble battle until the very end.

Believing that you can make something happen is not at all a small thing when you believe, add faith to yourself and speak to an expected end. What the mind sees, it says, and the body will follow. It is a chain reaction. Don't believe me...STOP: take a look at your current situation and think about what you've said previously about it. Then try and remember why you said the things that you said about your current situation. Look how your attitude and words have been revealed right before your eyes. This is one law of life that works every time with consistency of effort.

When people see that their Leader believes and strives hard for accomplishing a task, they will do the same. Imagine, if a single believer can make something happen, then how much more productivity can occur if the team, believers and do what they see in the Leader?

BRINGING OUT THE POSITIVE PERSON IN YOU

Leader, you must have a good attitude towards self. You cannot give to others what you do not have. So you always see the glass half-empty. But you know what? Even if half of the water spills on the floor, it still contains water, and it is half full! You will find something good in everything when you take the time to look. This normally involves getting YOU off of your mind and valuing the needs, ideas and opinions of others over your own. OUCH!!!…you can do it. Here are few ideas the that will anchor your attitude and change the attitude of the people around you:

1. **Keep your mind focused on important things.** Life is full of distractions, the best way to limit this beast is to write stuff down and make it visible. Visual reminders add the positive touch to keep your mind focused on the solution and your attitude positive. Your positive, peaceful and optimistic attitude is instrumental as you set goals and priorities that support your vision and mission. Visualize the end at the beginning. Program and plan the steps required to meet your expected end. Develop an effective strategy that anticipates and deals with potential problems in advance of occurrence. In other words, be proactive verses reactive. Focus on those things that will produce the greatest return; delegate and oversee the rest. Throughout, maintain a positive attitude knowing that you never begin anything with failure in mind.

2. :p **a list of your goals and actions.** Familiarize irself with long and short-term goals. Formulate ision points. Use the decision points to gage what ions to take given progress or lack thereof, during et period of time. Also, gage the progress of the m, encouraging them with words that relay your preciation of their efforts.

3. **detached from the outcome.** But take responsibility : the outcome. We start out with the end always in nd, but the gift of a positive attitude allows you project, plan, execute and see if and when change vay from the original plan is warranted. The people no fail at living a fulfilled life are the ones who main in a state of, "We've always done it this way." s the world changes and modern technology evolves, eaders must maintain the position where change not always evil, but may be a necessary evil. Your ttitude during these times will directly impact the ttitude of those you lead. This is one of those times vhen you want to complain, but silence is your best riend, and will produce a much better return.

Balance your desires. As a Leader, your team does not need to know that you are having personal issues. Your personal affairs should not impact your professional position. Fix your personal stuff first! Life takes a considerable amount of balance for Leaders. You have a life that is worthy of imitating. However, what is it telling your family, friends and team? It sh have the same message of love and appreciation, it has a different message to all three categories. real question is, what is your life saying to you. 've in a place of opposites – hot and cold, on anc, win and lose, happiness and sadness, pleasure ;pain, tears and laughter, love and hate. This is how cycle of life goes, but this is also a by-product of thoices that we make. Live every day as if it were ; last, with an attitude of making a difference, yet rining at peace and fulfilled.

5. **Be realistic.** Your expectations must be reac for your people to understand. However, ulistic expectations are not always a bad idea, especiawhen they force you and your team to stretch. Keepmind that without vision, knowledge and undersding, the wrong attitude may surface until positivsults are known. Bottom-line is that your people: not you, and it is your job to train them up in way that they should go - go out and represent yctheir Leader of Excellence.

6. **Create your environment.** Get around thowho have your solution and stay away from those whave your problem. Talk and share ideas with accomshed leaders outside of your inner circle. Do ι be intimidated, but rather take the nuggets of vlom received and expose your environment to newleas.

Become comfortable being outside of your comfort zone. Seek out optimistic examples that will fortify your self-confidence and self-esteem.

7. **Ask questions.** Children were blessed with the annoying thousand-question gift that most adults lose to early in life. It's annoying to you, but it's feeding a child's hunger and thirst for information. Knowledge is gained from the information; understanding from knowledge and wisdom from the repetition of those things that you understand. Ask questions. Questions do not equate to dumbness and ignorance; rather, it is the failure to ask the "right" questions that lead to dumbness and ignorance. Leaders are learners, sharers and receivers of information. You don't want to arrive at a level where you think that you know all that there is to know. You will not be a benefit to your team. Your people require you to stretch in order for them to grow so ask questions.

8. **Use what you have.** Focus on what you have rather than what you do not have. Everyone has a start, which sometimes is a long way from what they have developed over time. Once you solidify what you have to work with, walk in a spirit of gratitude. Adding on has much more value when your foundation is solid. Positive outcomes further emerge when you understand that you are not meant to do life alone. Most successful people love to tell their "ladder

49

climbing" stories. You too can start your own climb at home, and expand your dream only after you've closed the comparison gap that is discouraging you from starting to climb. Bet on you and maintain an optimistic attitude as you build successful results with great expectation.

*It is a terrible thing to see and
have no vision.*

HELEN KELLER

COMING IN AT ⑥

A LEADER MUST HAVE
VISION

A Leader's ability to be a Thinker, able to see the Big Picture, is imperative to sustaining a growth environment. An original thought apart from Internet search engines is the primary source for evolutionary Vision. Don't get me wrong, the search engines serve a wonderful purpose; they are filled with resources and ideas that you may never have considered. Mastermind groups are another source for bringing clarity to a vision. However, it is the dependency on another person's thoughts that limit the Leader's ability to cast the right vision at the right time, and into the hearts and minds of those being led. Vision is an indispensible leadership quality.

Casting a vision for your organization should be effective, useful, measurable and doable so that success by all is inevitable. Success is achieved at the start. It starts with you, the Leader. Once people buy into you as their Leader, they give value to your vision. The more that the vision gives the appearance of being for the benefit of others, the more it will be received by others as their own. Purpose and passion are keys to vision. If you know your purpose and are working in your passion, vision has no limits, and will keep you dreaming.

Therefore, to be an effective Leader, person of influence, you must have integrity and a vision. Without an example of promise, a clear vision of what you expect to accomplish and a roadmap for where you would like to go, no hope creates an environment for confusion.

BRINGING OUT THAT VISION IN YOU

To develop a vision, look within yourself. Vision comes from your inner self, your thoughts and dreams. Hence, your thoughts and dreams are a by-product of what you have been giving your attention to, which you have been receiving from and what you believe to be true about you.

Vision does not come suddenly like a magic trick, as some people seem to believe. It grows from the Leader's past experiences and is drawn on your talents, purpose and desires. Look to your source of peace where others stand to benefit from the vision given to you. After all of the parts and pieces line up, then it is time to do as the Bible says

"... 'Write the vision and make it plain on tablets, that he may run who reads it'."

HABAKKUK 2:2

When you finally have that vision that is indispensable to your leadership, don't just end there. Write it down and make if plain for those who are reading it to receive it as if it were their own. This is where your ability to influence begins.

Casting your vision to your people involves five steps:

1. **Listen.** Since vision starts within, you have to listen and know what your mind and heart really want. What stirs your heart? What is your greatest desire? What do you dream about? What is your passion? If what you wish to pursue does not actually come from the inner depths of you, it will be difficult, if not impossible, to achieve it.

   On the other hand, in fulfilling a greater vision, you need a good team to support you. Nobody can accomplish big things alone. Hence, seek out and listen to good advice from successful, more experienced Leaders in your field of interest. Hire a coach so that you may not be the lid to your own organization. There is nothing is wrong in asking for guidance. Great Leaders are perpetual learners and remain growth minded.

   Lastly, you should not be confined within your limited capabilities. A truly valuable vision must be coupled with faith.

2. **Prepare your mind.** As previously stated, the process of casting a vision begins with you, the Leader. The vision of your organization begins in your mind and heart.

It is something that you can feel, taste, see, hear, and touch with your soul. However, the defining moment of your vision is found in your faith. Your vision must be greater than your past memories, mistakes and accomplishments. It's developed in the hope that you can thinker greater than what you see, taste, touch, smell and taste. Your vision provides direction and is a guide throughout the journey. It keeps you focused in the face of adversity and rejection. Dissatisfaction and discouragement are not caused by the absence of practice, but by the absence of vision. Warren Bennis, author of *The Leadership Institute*, even said, **"Leadership is the capacity to translate vision into reality."**

The best way for your vision to become clear in your mind and heart is to reflect, retreat to a quiet and tranquil place – somewhere that will allow your mind to think creatively and solidify the vision as reality.

3. **Ask questions.** Great leaders recognize that they do not know everything. Always ask questions? This does not mean that you have to accept the answer as the truth, but if you do not ask, the truth has no chance to manifest in your ability to lead. Additionally, introduce your people to thought provoking questions that will help them see the vision and envision their participation in their heart, as being vital to mission accomplishment. Here are some suggested questions:

> ➤ Do you know the organization's vision, and if so, do you feel that you play an important role? Why or why not?

> ➤ What is one thing that you would change as the boss in support of the vision?

> ➤ Are there any areas within the organization that do not support the vision?

> ➤ What dreams inspire you?

4. **Identify the problem.** During this step, discuss with your team the challenges that may be keeping the required solutions identified by answering the above questions from manifesting. At the end of the day, this is not a fault-finding activity. After discussing potential challenges, take each one individually and discuss potential solutions. Awareness of the problem should always lead to solution identification.

5. **Proceed to a solution.** Overcoming problems will add immediate value to your vision and enlighten employees to the importance of accomplishing objectives and maintaining a unified vision. In this step you share your heart's vision and get the opinions and agreement of your leadership team. Everyone must be convinced that the solution will assist the organization to accomplish its mission and manifest your vision. It is very important at this point to ensure that the vision is plain, easily understood, measurable and adds value to others.

"Character makes trust possible. And trust makes Leadership possible."

JOHN C. MAXWELL

COMING IN AT (5)

A Leader Must Be TRUST Worthy

Trust is the most important factor in building effective relationships. My mentor John Maxwell also says that, "Trust is the Foundation of Leadership." Trust goes hand and hand with character and is the platform for your ability to effectively lead others. If you always remember that anything built on a lie is a temporary solution that will not last, you will always possess the key that unlocks another person's ability to trust in the genuine Leader in you.

Activist Barbara Smith stated that, "Trust is to human _relationships_ what faith is to gospel living. It is the beginning place, the _foundation_ upon which more can be built. Where trust is, love can flourish." All great Leaders desire to win the heart of their followers before asking for a hand. This one accomplishment alone transfers motive from self-fulfilling efforts into team effort.

Trust must be built. It is earned by consistent, confident competence, character and connection between Leader and Follower. When Followers trust the Leader, they tend to allow room for growth and excuse incidents when leadership may not have been at its best. However, this is only achieved through the consistent character of the Leader.

Character is without a doubt the number one trust blocker. Many Leaders have fallen abruptly from the top due to character flaws. Competence can only take you so far, yet compromise of character will push you back to the beginning, where you may never start again. Followers connect to the person who has their best interest at hand; and character is proof of the Leader's potential. Their trust is in the fact that the person that is leading them sees them and appreciates them as a valued contributor to the Leader's dream. It is, therefore, the Leader's responsibility to make decisions and exhibit character that is worth imitating.

Trust implies accountability (being responsible to other people or things), certainty (being confident and assured), and reliability (being able to be depended on due to accuracy). It must be developed every time, while remaining cautious in handling it.

Ever heard the cliché: *It takes a long period of time to build trust and only seconds to break it?*

Beware of actions that can easily betray trust like the following:

> ➤ breaking promises (over and over again)
> ➤ showing favoritism

➤ divulging Follower-trusted information to others, without permission

➤ creating discord amongst your people/gossiping

Remember that trust is the bond that makes the relationship between you (as a Leader) and your people last. Build it wisely, and expect it to last.

How to Bring Out the Trustworthy Person in You

1. **Be yourself.** When you allow other people to see the real "you," they will drop the barriers and accept you. They too will open up and appreciate your Leadership as a gift, and not as a job. However, know that you are actually three people: the person that you believe that you are, the person that others perceive you to be, and the person that you really are. It is your goal in life to make sure that that all three people become one. It is at this point that your actions and words produce the greatest leadership results.

2. **Pursue lifelong learning.** Leaders are learners. Have a desire to continually learn and grow both personally and professionally. Remain open to new ideas and continuously seek knowledge that can help you grow and make rewarding impact in the lives of others. Learn how to expand your thinking, while maintaining a broad focus of things around you. In the Army we call this "Situational Awareness."

Be honest with you - Success is a team sport. Andrew Carnegie says that, "It marks a big step in your development when you come to realize that other people can help you do a better job than you can do alone." Taking classes, attending conferences, asking for help is NOT a sign of weakness, it is wise to have mature counsel; and it's OK to sometimes be the dumbest person in the room. This approach raises the lid over your life and opens up your mind to thoughts that you alone would never have.

3. **Admit your faults.** The 'truth' is the greatest, most rewarding and respected gift that a leader possesses. Your admission of fault may not fix the problem, but it will be appreciated more than you can imagine. The problem is that most Leaders focus on the problem, while great Leaders focus on the solution. **Your admission of fault immediately shifts the focus when followed up with a plan of action.** DO NOT make excuses. Excuses are the tool of the uncommitted. Your commitment to a better outcome is clearly stated when the failure goes unjustified. Leaders delegate authority, but we keep responsibility; therefore, even in the case of your trusted agent's failure, Leaders maintain responsibility for the outcome and DO NOT blame other people. This does not mean that no one will suffer the consequences for their actions. It only means that great Leaders assess their role in the

outcome, and render appropriate correction that will prevent the same type of outcome in the future.

4. **Listen.** Leaders have an obligation to hear, and to hear right. Your people have a voice and should be heard. Anticipate the needs of your people. They sometimes talk in actions instead of words. Listening does not always constitute agreement, but it is a great tool for developing trust. Honest, well thought out feedback assures your people that they are a valued commodity to the big picture. Repeat what you hear and assure the person doing the talking that you're actually listening. Keep a pad handy, take notes and follow-up when required.

5. **Get to know the people on your team**. Host social events for you team, and have opportunities where family members may participate. Develop and spend personal time with your inner-circle. Staff retreats are a great tool to accomplish team building. Be visible. Ask questions. KNOW THE NAMES OF YOUR PEOPLE. If you have a large company/organization, make it mandatory for your supervisor's to know their Followers name, as they are imitating your example. Institute a monthly birthday and/or anniversary celebration and unlock the barrier that allows relationship to develop. Offer opportunities and rewards for volunteering outside of your organization. Most importantly, pay attention to personality changes.

"Character is what one is; reputation is what one is thought to be by others."

COMING IN AT ④

A LEADER MUST HAVE STRENGTH OF
CHARACTER

According to my mentor, John C. Maxwell, author of *Leadership 101* and *Developing the Leaders around You*, the first thing to look for in any kind of Leader or potential Leader is their strength of character: "I have found nothing more important than this quality."

First, we need to define character. Merriam-Webster dictionary defines character as 'one of the attributes that make-up and distinguish an individual.' D. L. Moody said, "Character is what you are in the dark." Moody's definition actually is defining character as what you really are when no one is looking, and not the refined representative that you allow others to see. Character is what guides your actions and produces the words you speak. Character is your unique identity, your personality; the sum total of your individual characteristics.

Character can be good or bad. Strength of character refers to the strong and good character. A person strong in character is someone who consistently stands for what is right, who has the "courage" to express and live out personal convictions. However, the true character of a person is revealed under pressure when opportunity arises to do what's right or please people.

The qualities that make up good character are honesty, integrity, devotion, self-discipline, determination, dependability, perseverance, conscientiousness, patience, a strong work ethic, a spirit of excellence and a servant leader. A person with right character does what they say, and says what they do, regardless of being seen. Their reputation is solid and consistent. They have respect for themselves, their family, and their nation. Their example is worthy of replication.

As there is no perfect person in the world, all of us are what I like to refer to as, works in progress, growing in the qualities mentioned above. These qualities are essential and must not to be ignored. History continues to reveal how character flaws will eventually make a Leader ineffective – every time. Hence, if you notice any of the following characteristics and behaviors below, you may be negatively impacting your potential to be an effective Leader:

> consistently late and unprepared

> prideful, not able to complete tasks and refuse to seek assistance

> undone obligations and broken promises

> not taking responsibility for your actions

> failure to meet deadlines and making excuses for failure

> being oversensitive to criticisms and comments

> self-seeking and critical of others

Intentionally take control of your actions and develop the right character traits. Changing character flaws is a process that must take root in your heart first, in order to change your attitude and actions. It's an inward process that produces outward results.

Bringing Out that Strong Character in You

As the Leader, the one who influences others, you are the one that people see. People do what people see. Therefore, if you're not seeing proper character traits in your team, take a self-assessment, make the changes and teach your team to do the same. You are the example, the role model, and now is the time to show your team what right looks like. If you're not sure what right looks like, get an accountability partner, someone who genuinely cares about you, to stretch you. In other words, look outside of self and see what right looks like in the lives of others.

1. **Believe in yourself.** Before you expect anybody else to believe in you, you should be the first person to believe in who you are and in what you can do. Look at and see yourself the way you want others to see you. If you want others to respect you, learn to respect yourself. If you want others to love you, love yourself first. Focus

on the things you do well and try to develop areas where you are weak.

2. **Engage in training**. Leaders are learners. It's not always the technical areas that require development; the relational areas require development too. If you know that you're weak in a specific area, intentionally exercise your ability to succeed in that area. For instance, if you know that you lack patience, and patience is needed to strengthen your character in other areas, exercise patience by getting in long lines, allow the couple behind you to be serviced before you, etc.

3. **Develop mental toughness.** One of the joys of leadership is found in a Leader's ability to withstand persecution, criticism and rejection. Your ability to lead above the opinions of others is key to your success. You must be mentally tough, as your ability to do right and represent excellence is not always appreciated. A tough-minded Leader knows how to remain focused, accepting that which is good, and rejecting that which is not. They know how to adjust, adapt and overcome. Welcome constructive criticism as an opportunity for improvement. Learn from mistakes and never be oversensitive.

4. **Follow right examples.** Even Leaders need a mentor, a model of integrity and leadership. Keep your environment filled with people smarter than you, possessing strong qualities, and character traits that

you would want to imitate. Go where the examples are: sign up for their newsletters; attend their events; step out in faith, make an appointment and ask questions. Don't limit your examples, there are plenty out there, but narrow the scope to those capable of speaking into your future.

Although, I've served in the U.S. Army as an officer for over 23 years, upon retirement, I joined the John Maxwell Team, having received from John's consistent example of excellence in industry. I am confident, that as I write this book, imitating John's quality leadership traits will continue to be instrumental in my success in leadership outside of the Army.

5. **Display integrity.** Integrity is another key ingredient to a Leader's ability to influence others. If your actions and words do not line up, it creates trust issues. In order for followers to be the most productive, they must know that the Leader's word and actions are one. Your ability to be authentic, reliable and competent are the connecting factor for a leader and the led. Your integrity resonates a sense of hope, care and concern, and followers require to know that they are adding value to something and/or someone who represents good.

Do not hesitate to assess your integrity through the feedback of mentors, as well as, through organizational climate surveys. You can ultimately be your best and worst critic; choose wisely.

"*Success is like a game of basketball; you can only get so far by yourself.*"

COMING IN AT ③

A LEADER MUST BE
INFLUENTIAL

Michael Jordan is undeniably one of the greatest basketball players of all time. However, with numerous individual accomplishments and awards, it was the leadership of his Head coach, Phil Jackson that gave Michael his greatest accomplishments and the Chicago Bulls their most memorable victories. Coach Jackson instituted a triangle offense that created a system for all five players on the floor to score; yet giving Michael free reign to score as plays broke down. Almost seven years after Michael was drafted by the NBA it was Jackson's leadership that influenced this phenomenal basketball player to generate synergy with his teammates, resulting in six NBA championships.

Influence is the core of leadership. It is the foundation for which greatness derives. Your ability to lead others toward Specific, Measureable, Attainable, Realistic and Timely (SMART) goals, is dependent on your ability to influence. Position, title and name will only produce temporary results, which are normally forgotten in the absence of the Leader. If

71

you ever want to test your ability to influence, you should have children.

After six failed pregnancies', it was the seventh pregnancy, and birth of my son, my eighth child and only child, that truly tested and solidified my ability to lead. Leading in the Army for over 23 years has nothing on being an active, participatory, single parent of a male man-child. You would think that after finally succeeding in such a wonderful feat, I'd be up to the assignment. Right! We, Parent, Leaders, have a responsibility to raise up our children in the way that they should go. However, our future Leaders come into this world with their own agenda and no pressure of not receiving a paycheck. Breaking the barrier of "Me" and "Mines" has proven quite challenging, yet the power of influence prevails. I will admit, it is definitely a slow process where the many definitions of love get in the way of correction. Nevertheless, as a Leader, the ability to influence your children into greatness that supersedes your wildest expectations is truly the best gift of all times; as they grow and imitate what they see in you.

Influence is more than telling people what to do. Just like our children, people will do what they see first and ask questions later. You are the example, and it is your duty to make sure that your example is worth imitating. People need your influence.

Most people do their jobs out of life's obligations. They perform in exchange of a salary they need for everyday living.

However, if these people were under a Leader who had an effective influence over them, they would do their job because they want to…because they are able to learn from doing it, and because they know that it is for the attainment of the team's goal. If the Leader is influential people will follow their Leader's instructions gladly and confidently, even without any material incentive,.

ACTIVATING THE INFLUENCER IN YOU

As a Leader, you cannot give what you do not have. You cannot lead where you don't know; although you can navigate to where you've never been. Leaders must be able to relay their team what the expected end looks like. Followers are more supportive of Leaders who know where they are going, and have understanding of how long it will take to get there. Followers must know that their time is not being wasted. Great influencers develop relationships, resulting in Followers who follow the Leader 1st and mission 2nd. Here are a few techniques for developing your ability to influence.

1. **Assess your people.** Leaders should know their people. Depending on the size of your organization, you should, at a minimum, know the names of the spouses of your employees. It is the personal touches that allow your people to connect with you as a person. Look for their potential. Find out their strengths and weaknesses. Develop what they have and equip them with solutions to offset their weaknesses. Getting to

know your people is how they recognize your genuine care and concern. This is also what moves them from a place of working for you to working *with* you. Working with you is far less stressful than working for you. Other factors to look for include skills and abilities, educational background, dreams and desires, family values and leadership potential.

2. **Grow them with your words.** A great Leaders know how to communicate and connect with their people effectively. Use words that build up and not tear down. Even in the midst of correction, identify the problem, their role played in creating the incident; render the consequences, if any, and end with words that outline how to prevent such an occurrence from happening again. Then ask for their support of your request. Always appreciate your people with your words and actions.

3. **Have courage.** A Leader must be courageous. You must be prepared to go where others will not dare, and stand when others have fallen. Leaders must make difficult decisions in the face of opposition and ridicule, with confidence, accepting responsibility for those decisions. Followers look to the Leader to make the right decisions. They do not want or respect a timid Leader who makes inconsistent decisions. Indecisiveness will soon result in loss of faith in you, your vision and your ability to lead. They want

someone to lead them, someone who will take full responsibility for the decisions made. At the end of the day, people just want to know that they support a leader who supports them and will not compromise.

4. **Develop peer respect.** Peer respect involves character and personality between you and your people. Trammell Crow, one of the world's most successful real estate brokers, said that he looks for people whose associates want them to succeed. He said, "It's tough enough to succeed when everybody wants you to succeed. People who don't want you to succeed are like weights in your running shoes." On the other hand, Maxey Jarmen used to say, "It isn't important that people like you. It's important that they respect you. They may like you but not follow you. If they respect you, they'll follow you, even if perhaps they don't like you."

5. **Empower.** An effective Leader sets clear objectives for his team members, but leaves detailed implementation of these objectives to the discretion and judgment of individual members of the team. As Second World War U.S. General George S. Patton puts it, "Don't tell people how to do things. Tell them what to do and let them surprise you with their results." I don't know about surprising me with results, but I definitely encourage in-progress reviews throughout the process to ensure that milestones are being met and that effort

supports the objective.

6. **Authenticity.** I am a member of the John Maxwell Team, which comes with an internationally known mentor, in John, and various direct contact coaches from around the world. My followers may recognize and associate my abilities with the John Maxwell brand; however, at the end of the day they desire that I be an authentic Leader. Your ability to influence is anchored in the accurate representation of you. Your authenticity is what will last, and what will lead.

7. **Availability.** Make dedicated time to meet the needs and concerns of your people. Let it be known that you care and are open to leader-subordinate interaction. Do not be afraid to ask for or receive feedback. When faced with negative comments, do not take them personal. If the comments are true, fix it, and I would love to say, if they're false, trash it. However, even false comments have a root cause. Perception is reality to the one who perceived it as true. It pays great dividends to locate the source of the negative comment and deal with it accordingly. In other words, do not just blow it off.

8. **Follow up.** Check work in progress, and identify milestones that identify expectation at specific periods of time where decisions must be made to continue, cancel, adjust, or replace. Stay visible to your people,

providing compliments, as well as, corrections. Train your people to meet suspense dates, and/or request assistance prior to missing the suspense. You can catch potential problems, in advance by checking up early.

"Law of the Picture: People do what people see."

JOHN C. MAXWELL

COMING IN AT ②

A LEADER MUST BE
DISCIPLINED

An effective Leader is also a follower. We all follow something or someone; therefore, I started a company that teaches Leaders to follow the truth. There are facts and there is the truth, the truth is the only thing that will last. Facts change and anything built on a lie will eventually be exposed. Following the truth definitely takes discipline, as following a lie tends to be easier and easier for most. The Leader is the first person that is led. Thus, if you, the Leader, expect your people to be disciplined, you must be the first one to possess this character trait, as well as, the traits that you expect to see in your people. Once you discipline yourself to do what is right, you now have the right to correct and or discipline others. If you fail to be disciplined and or discipline, you give up the right to complain. **"Never complain about what you permit."**

In the midst of uncertainty there is unrest. Followers begin to reach their own conclusions, directly impacting their behavior. Who do you blame when the behavior is a direct result of what is seen in you, the Leader. Should punishment be rendered? The truth is, punishment tends to be rendered when day-to-day mentoring/training supports outcome. We must fix this. Life without restrictions is pandemonium. Discipline has the power to transform the unknown to the known, confusion into peace and the lost into found.

As a U.S. Army officer, I've been conditioned to value the importance of time, being on time and how it impacts others. In a business and field of work where life and death decisions are required, self-discipline is not optional. However, in any business environment, self-discipline is also not optional as others are depending on your leadership to lead them. Self-discipline presents an atmosphere saturated with confidence...confidence that you and your word are one. It presents an atmosphere of trust. Most importantly, it presents an atmosphere where you the Leader, are viewed as a great example of someone to imitate.

Do what I say and NOT as I do! Most people follow the instructions out of obligation, antagonism and anger. These are not good leadership traits for a Great Leader. We live in society where your neighbor comes from a different walks of life. A self-disciplined Leader is the one connecting factor that navigates followers in a multi-faceted environment. As a Leader, it is your duty and responsibility to discipline the people you manage. You will not be able to complete this assignment unless you are a disciplined citizen yourself.

Bringing Out the Disciplined Individual in You

Self-discipline starts inside out. Being disciplined is more than just controlling your temper or being prepared and on time for appointments. It is rooted and grounded in you purposely being the best you...physically, mentally, socially, professionally, and spiritually. Here are some self-development tools that will focus you to grow in this area of leadership.

1. **Control your emotions.** You are a product of what you give your attention to. Guard your mind in order to project affirmative thoughts especially when fear arises. Reverse negative thoughts immediately. Affirmative thoughts constitute controlled emotions.

2. **Be patient.** Impatience is a sign of immaturity. You should not dig up seeds just to see whether they are growing. Cultivate ideas and desires, execute them, and patiently wait for the fruits of your labor to manifest.

3. **Do IT Right.** Don't just do IT, do it right! Do some research and find out what is available to help you plan and prepare more effectively. Choose planning tools that help you organize your meetings, appointments, tasks, projects, etc., in a consolidated manner. The best tools have more than one functionality. Whatever you do, do not become so comfortable, that you prefer more work over change. The slightest process enhancement can either delay or accelerate your

vision. Making the right process enhancements will keep you from experiencing a Redo.

4. **Work-out a systematic plan for each goal.** Take one task at a time and complete it. However, for those of us who are Big Picture thinkers - we see the pieces and parts while simultaneously managing the big picture as a whole. We are blessed to do more than one thing at a time. This gift requires strategic prioritization. You can only move effectively in one direction at one time; therefore, you need a strategic plan to ensure that movement at every level continues to take place. Discipline yourself to the accomplishment of the true No. 1 priority before moving on to the next.

5. **Expect to give up to go up.** Discipline requires sacrifice. Discipline requires tunnel vision. A familiar phrase often used refers to our ability to manage time; however, in reality, you cannot manage time. It is a constant and cannot be added to or subtracted from. The Truth is that we must manage ourselves in relation to time. In order to be successful, you will not be able to afford the luxury of laziness or the delights of frequent distraction. Unless you are willing to make the required sacrifices, you are just wasting your time.

6. **Be persistent.** Great Leaders maintain a Victory mindset. Failure is not an option, but instead, a delay to success. The greatest Leaders became who they

are today because when falling and/or stumbling along their journey, they did not quit, but made the appropriate adjustments and kept moving forward. *A man was digging for gold. He became frustrated, gave up and walked away. He left the shovel in the ground, and a short while later, another man came along, picked up the shovel and starting digging. He dug six more feet and hit a major vein of gold! The first man gave up six feet too soon!* DO NOT have this testimony!

7. **Stop making excuses!** Excuses are the enemy to Leaders. They serve to prevent, delay and limit. Excuses are also the tool of the uncommitted. Excuses are contagious and are often shared by those that you lead. As long as you are not 100% committed, you will not achieve 100% results. To become a more disciplined person, you must destroy self-limiting thoughts and self-talk. As George Bernard Shaw once said, *"I don't believe in circumstances. The people who get on in this world are the people who look for the circumstances they want, and if they can't find them, they make them."* No more excuses!

"Faith is taking the first step even when you don't see the whole staircase."

MARTIN LUTHER KING, JR.

COMING IN AT ①

A LEADER MUST HAVE FAITH

Don't panic...Keep reading! A Leader's ability to exercise faith is not a religious attempt to conform you. Faith comes from a place of "knowing" and is a law that works through love. If you truly love you, and what you do, faith is your greatest asset. Therefore, see you in your future today and do something about it!

The principle of faith has its roots from that which does not exist; however, we have the ability to dream BIG, believe and see tomorrow, in today. Hebrews 11:1 describes as "Now faith is the substance of things hoped for, the evidence of things not seen." Faith is the substance that reveals what you can't comprehend with your 5 senses. It is the evidence that your passion, dreams and desires are a reality. As a Leader, if you wait for tomorrow before planning today, tomorrow has a limited chance of success. *"No matter how much you learn from the past, it will never tell all that is required for success in the future."* Dream big.

A Leader's faith does not have to be as infinitely big as the galaxies are to the size of the Earth. It just has to be as infinitely big as the galaxies are to the size of the Earth inside of you. As the Hubble Space Telescope reveals the magnificence of the heavens above, your works and your words reveal the magnificence of your faith to others.

Put Your Faith to the Test. Faith is anchored by Trust, sustained by Hope, realized through Patience and manifested by Perseverance. It is the one friend that will have you sleeping comfortably when most would be awake with worry. Faith teaches you to listen more, talk less and work wiser.

1. **Faith is Contagious.** Faith will have you to place multi-million dollar facility schematics throughout your three person office, and move your two employees to host frequent conversations about "when we move." Visualize what the end result will look like. Writing a clear detailed vision will force you and others to see on the outside what you've visualized on the inside. It allows you to work backwards in your mind as you pursue the tasks required to move from today into tomorrow. Ask yourself the tough questions: What value does my vision add to the Big Picture called life? Why me and is what I'm believing for necessary? Is my faith for something that will benefit anyone other than me? Am I up to the challenge of leading my team and persevering in the face of opposition? Ask your people questions to ensure that what you have faith

for is what they see. Welcome their input and celebrate in advance as your Followers start dreaming on your behalf. Imagine. Anticipate. Prepare.

2. **Faith requires Patience.** Although the vision is 20/20 clear to you, it may require a substantial amount of time to materialize. Practicing patience will open your mind up to additional ways to best use your resources to move things along. It focuses you to make the right decisions at the right time, verses emotional decisions that always result in regret. Patience may require you to change your environment and take a walk in the park, go for a run, spend time alone to reflect in order to strategically plan -- whatever works for you. Setting time aside to think will tremendously enhance your ability to think and remain patient. Record your thoughts and follow-up to ensure that your patience remains a necessity of the process and not the result of poor planning.

3. **Faith requires Vision.** What do you see? Where are you looking? Who and what you give your attention to is instrumental in what you see in your mind's eye. Leaders must see what they expect to see in the future, now. We live in a world of endless possibilities that may be obtained by faith because you believe. There is nothing impossible to great Leaders that believe. However, without faith, possibilities soon become impossibilities, when you fail to pursue and share your

dreams. It is a Leader's duty to develop their people up to the level of the vision through the transfer of faith that works through love. This will only happen as a result of you, the Leader, reflecting confidence, faith and direction for what you're believing to occur.

Tradition and conformity are enemies of faith. They are by-products of doubt, unbelief, fear and worry. They actually hold the future hostage to the past. So as not to fall victim to public opinion and rejection, always see the end now, welcome rejection with optimism, welcome wise counsel, do not make comparisons, cast down unproductive thoughts and conversations, decorate your surroundings with reminders of your future, say what you want to see, never equate failure to self worth and never quit.

4. **Faith requires Navigation.** Yes navigation. How do you navigate the unknown? The unknown is unseen, unheard, unfelt, has no smell or taste, yet by faith it has a date with destiny; that's only if you add some works to your faith. Adding works and words to faith produces results, just like the spirit to the body produces life. In other words, faith is perfected by works. An expecting mother does not wait until the baby is born before she prepares for the arrival. She begins to plan for feeding, clothing, cleaning, housing, transporting, and for all that is required to provide the best care prior to the birth of her baby. If you're expecting to hire more

employees, you go out and research a larger office space prior to hiring. If you're believing for a new car, you "should" clean out the garage prior to even looking at vehicles. As a Leader, have the same commitment to your people. If you envision an ever evolving business, organization, church, etc., you must start instituting plans and processes that are best suited to receive your vision in the future, now.

As stated throughout this book, great Leaders see the big picture. Their focus is not moved by temporary setbacks. Faith allows Leaders to see today, and know that the concerns of today carry no weight in tomorrow. Faith keeps you **solution focused and not problem intimidated**, and will navigate you to your end results without a map.

5. **Faith requires Integrity.** If you want what you are believing for to be a reality in the hearts and minds of others, your words and actions must be ONE. Integrity takes the guesswork out of the unknown for others. Integrity is the one quality that establishes the foundation for the other leadership qualities. Integrity produces lasting results as it moves the unknown to the known in the hearts and minds of others.

CONCLUSION

So, you've read my top 12 qualities and yes I do have others that make me a great leader. While my number one quality may be my true number one leadership quality, the order of qualities is not what I would like for you to take away from this book. It's when you start living these principles and seeing them manifest in the lives of others, leadership is at its best. Being a Leader is such a rewarding assignment...lots of responsibility, with plenty of opportunities to build relationships and make a difference in the lives of others who will do the same. Therefore, Leader, please discipline yourself to do what's right...because it's the right thing to do. Allow your life of integrity to speak for you in your absence, remain a person of influence that is worthy of imitation.

You have what it takes -- expect GREATNESS -- knowing that it is your expectation that determines your preparation. It is the preparation that dictates the confidence. It is the confidence that provides the attitude and enlightens the awareness of others who soon know that they are a part of a GREAT TEAM. Who wants to be on a losing team? The leadership qualities detailed in this book are just the beginning of your success. SUCCESS defined as *"an 'on purpose,' process of increased improvement that has the capability to add value to someone other than you."*

Always remember that:

A Leader must have Faith...

... A Leader's faith does not have to be as infinitely big as the galaxies are to the size of the Earth. It just has to be as infinitely big as the galaxies are to the size of the Earth inside of you. As the Hubble Space Telescope reveals the magnificence of the heavens above, your works and your words reveal the magnificence of your faith to others.

A Leader must be disciplined...

...Self-discipline presents an atmosphere saturated with confidence...confidence that you and your word are one. It presents an atmosphere of trust...Trust that what you say, you do. Most importantly, it presents an atmosphere where you the Leader, are viewed as a great example of someone to imitate.

A Leader must be influential...

...Influence is the core of leadership. It is the foundation for which greatness derives. Your ability to lead others toward Specific, Measureable, Attainable, Realistic and Timely (SMART) goals, is dependent on your ability to influence. Position, title and name will only produce temporary results, which are normally forgotten in the absence of the Leader.

A Leader must have strength of character...

...Character can be good or bad. Strength of character refers to the strong and good character. A person strong in character is someone who consistently stands for what is right, who has the "courage" to express and live out personal convictions. However, the true character of a person is revealed under pressure; when opportunity arises to do what's right or please people.

A Leader must be trust worthy...

...Trust goes hand and hand with character and is the platform for your ability to effectively lead others. If you always remember that anything built on a lie is a temporary solution that will not last, you will always possess the key that unlocks another person's ability to trust in the genuine Leader in you.

A Leader must have vision...

...Casting a vision for your organization should be effective, useful, measurable and doable so that success by all is inevitable. Success is achieved at the start. It starts with you, the Leader. Once people buy into you as their Leader, they give value to your vision.

A Leader must have a positive attitude...

...As a Leader, you must have a positive attitude towards yourself in order to project a positive attitude toward others. It's impossible to give others what you do not have. The beauty of attitude is that it's already inside of you, and you can control it.

A Leader must make a decision and be willing to take responsibility...

... It is imperative for a Leader to make a decision and take responsibility for that decision. It is the example of integrity that keeps great Leaders making the right decisions for the right reason and at the right time.

A Leader must have effective communication skills...

...Communication is the key to knowing, understanding and achieving success. An effective Leader must develop communication skills in order to communicate and connect with followers. It's not so much your ability to speak, as it is your ability to be heard and responded to. It's not so much your ability to hear, as it is your ability to effectively listen and see.

A Leader must be adaptable, willing to make changes...

...A great Leader knows how to adjust, adapt and overcome; they are willing to make necessary changes for the right reasons and for the good of the team. It is when Leaders fully understand their ability to impact their environment, that the environment is forced to submit to the leading of the "Agent of Change." Otherwise, you are merely one of the followers.

A Leader must be deliberate, knowing how and what to prioritize...

...Leaders must be deliberate and disciplined to prioritize while working towards specific goals. Knowing the what, when, where, why and how will make life as a Leader more consistent and focused. Being deliberate, forces Leaders to prioritize, all of the competing requirements that must be accomplished, by importance.

Finally, a Leader must be able to develop other Leaders...

... When a Leader fails to develop other leaders the Leader finds themselves doing all of the thinking and all of the work. This approach to Leadership is unnecessary, especially since the purpose of leading is to lead people.

The greatness of leadership is already inside of you, develop it and lead life to the fullest, making tremendous and rewarding impact in the lives of those looking forward to following you.

Alethes Consulting Group, LLC

"TRUTH Leads and Leaders Follow"
Notepad
www.alethesconsultinggroup.com
(240) 245-0503

TRAINING LEADERS WORLDWIDE

Alethes Consulting Group, LLC

"TRUTH Leads and Leaders Follow"
Notepad
www.alethesconsultinggroup.com
(240) 245-0503

TRAINING LEADERS WORLDWIDE

Alethes Consulting Group, LLC
"TRUTH Leads & Leaders Follow"

LEADER,

Thank you for choosing to live a life

that makes positive impact in the lives of others.

For additional information on any of the qualities,

philosophies, strategies and ideas used in this book,
please contact

Alethes Consulting Group, LLC

(240) 245-0503

email *info@alethesconsultinggroup.com*

and make an appointment for your

FREE

30-minute virtual consultation.

CONNECT with us online at:

➤ http://www.alethesconsultinggroup.com

➤ http://www.Facebook.com/AlethesConsulting

➤ Twitter: SG_SpeaksTruth

➤ Linkedin: Sharon D. Green

Alethes (AL-AY-THACE) is the Greek word for speaking the truth, loving the truth, authentic; in other words, nothing hidden